The Aging Twenty

Illustrations By Sebastian Lopez-Santiago

T. Goldwire LLC

Instagram: @ToniMGoldwire

ISBN: 978-0-578-69610-2

Library of Congress Number:

TXu002175479/2019-12-06

Edited by T. Rox

Art by Artist Sebastian Lopez-Santiago

I dedicate this book to
my parents Tony and Sunday.

Special Thanks:

To all those who were there with me during the journey of writing this book. Thank you and I love you!

Book Forward

Call me when you turn twenty-one....
twenty-three...
twenty-five…

Those words often echoed between my friends and me. I felt it my duty to provide a proper warning as to what was coming. You see, at twenty I was young, wild and free. With the perfect body and bouncy hair, I possessed an inner light that could light up the darkness of anyone who stared. Twenty was the perfect age!

The downfall about being twenty is the inevitable twenty-one, twenty-three and twenty-five. All pivotal moments indeed that possess a set of unique challenges to any twenty-something. These things all must be done while aging gracefully. Hence, the name The Aging Twenty. This book addresses a few of those challenges; from losing yourself to finding faith in the journey, along with the lessons learned along the way.

Book Forward

Through poetry and illustrations this book is set in the theme of a house. Each poem guides you through the many encounters a twenty-something will find along their journey. All the while, enduring the house they have theoretically built for themselves. You'll find their many adventures with fake friends, aging, mental health and various other relationships. I wrote this book for the twenty-year-old in all of us still fighting to get out in the world and let their unique light shine.

Fortunately, I had strong loving people by my side through the journey and for that I am forever grateful. However, many don't have that support system. So, I felt it only right to write this book for everyone amidst their blessing and struggling to make sense of it all. I'm just letting you know that you are not crazy and that you must keep going on your journey before you see the light. Keep fighting the fine fight, it gets better, I promise!

-T.Goldwire

Table Of Contents

Table Of Contents

Chapter 1:

Rental

Sold!

Alice Re-written

Currently, standing on the threshold
of my rabbit hole;
Mental fires, wait to be extinguished cold.

I stare into the darkness of my framework;
Wondering if maybe, these fires would
light my worth.

I'm afraid to step into this hole.
I start to forget where to place my feet;

I lose balance and I began to lose my faith.
My rabbit hole gets darker as I continue to
sprawl;

Unhinging everything, I installed, so
through this door, I began my freefall...

Rental

I was shining too bright, so
She offered to show me the way.
Taking me by the hand, she rented me this
Cute, little, minimalistic place
Convincing me it was the only way.

In turn, I rented someone else's
Mental space.
I begin to skinny down, suppressing
My baggage to just one crate.
Trimming the hedges and throwing on
A little paint.

Instead, every morning, the mirror
I seemed to break;
the reflected reflection of someone else's face.
Still, every morning, I'd make
The bed and clear my plate

Of old cheap TV dinners from yesterday
And sat at a table, where breakfast
I could no longer take.
Because in that moment, I realized
That's where I chose to stay.

Left Overs

Don't worry, just use the one from
yesterday, ok?
But, what about security?
Your fine, don't worry, just put it on
tomorrow's plate;
so, there went a large helping of meat
to stay.
But what of clarity?
Your fine, don't worry, just put it on
tomorrow's plate;
meanwhile, down went the mashed
potatoes.
You can't have clarity, without a little
anxiety
so on went the gravy I smothered.
But, what about my mental health?
Your fine, don't worry, just put it on
tomorrow's plate;
so seasoned French cuts were placed.
But what of my future?
Your fine, don't worry, just use the
one from yesterday.

Wall Clock

The hands of time
Discriminated against me
Wrapping me up in futility

Altering my young state of mind
Giving me the perception of forever
And mentally granting me invincibility

Only to discriminate against me physically

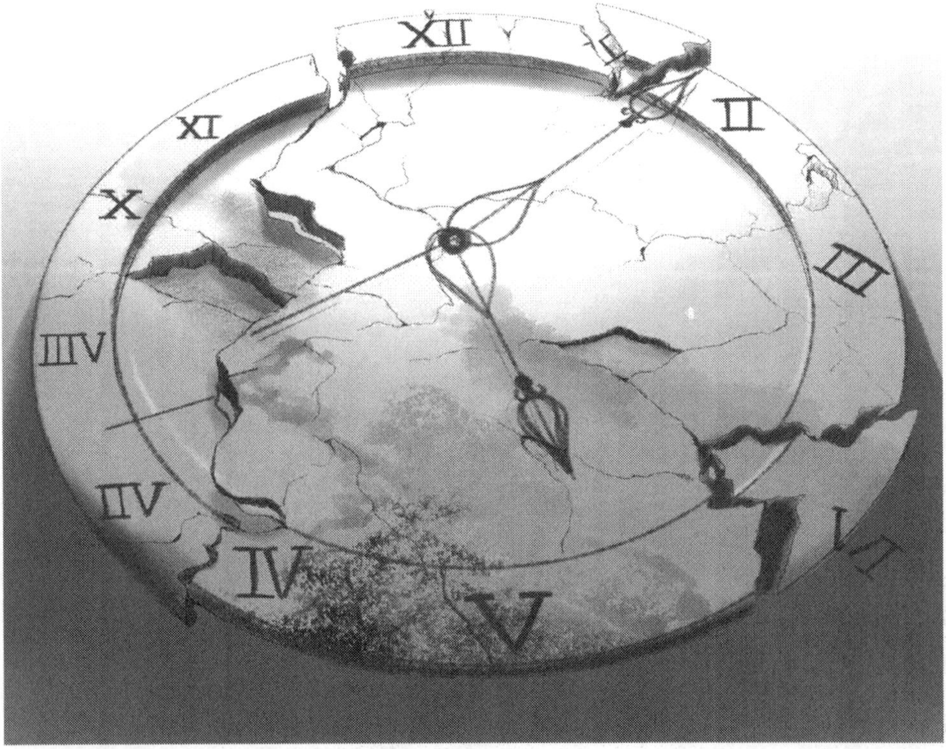

On Borrowed Time

I'm tired of being here
Depressed, by all these useless fears
        Will time stop?
To see, why my soul's been rocked?
Can time hold memories of the past?
        Far enough away to see,
why cymbals in my head clash
So, I can figure out why music hurts
        and classical music makes
        everything a blur
And why birds of my neighborhood won't chirp?
The door from winter to spring seems to be closed
        And why the weight of this
        season seems so cold?
I just need some time, to live in my now.
For I'm afraid;
                I'm breaking
                        down.

If It's Any Constellation

(The Beauty of Nightfall)

She said, “It's dark in here”.
She'd never seen me like this before.
If only she knew this is my daybreak,
she will never know
how dark it gets.

I'm distracted by a tumbling sound
I've stopped being rattled now.
I know it's just negative thoughts, ascending into my abyss,
Leftovers, from the previous droughts.

Continually she admits,
“I saw that sparkle you had,
your gift nobody seems to get -- Love.
Its sparkle seems to no longer exist,
your light I'm starting to miss”

“I can barely see you now.
Does your heart still pound?
I love you, I hope you know this”.

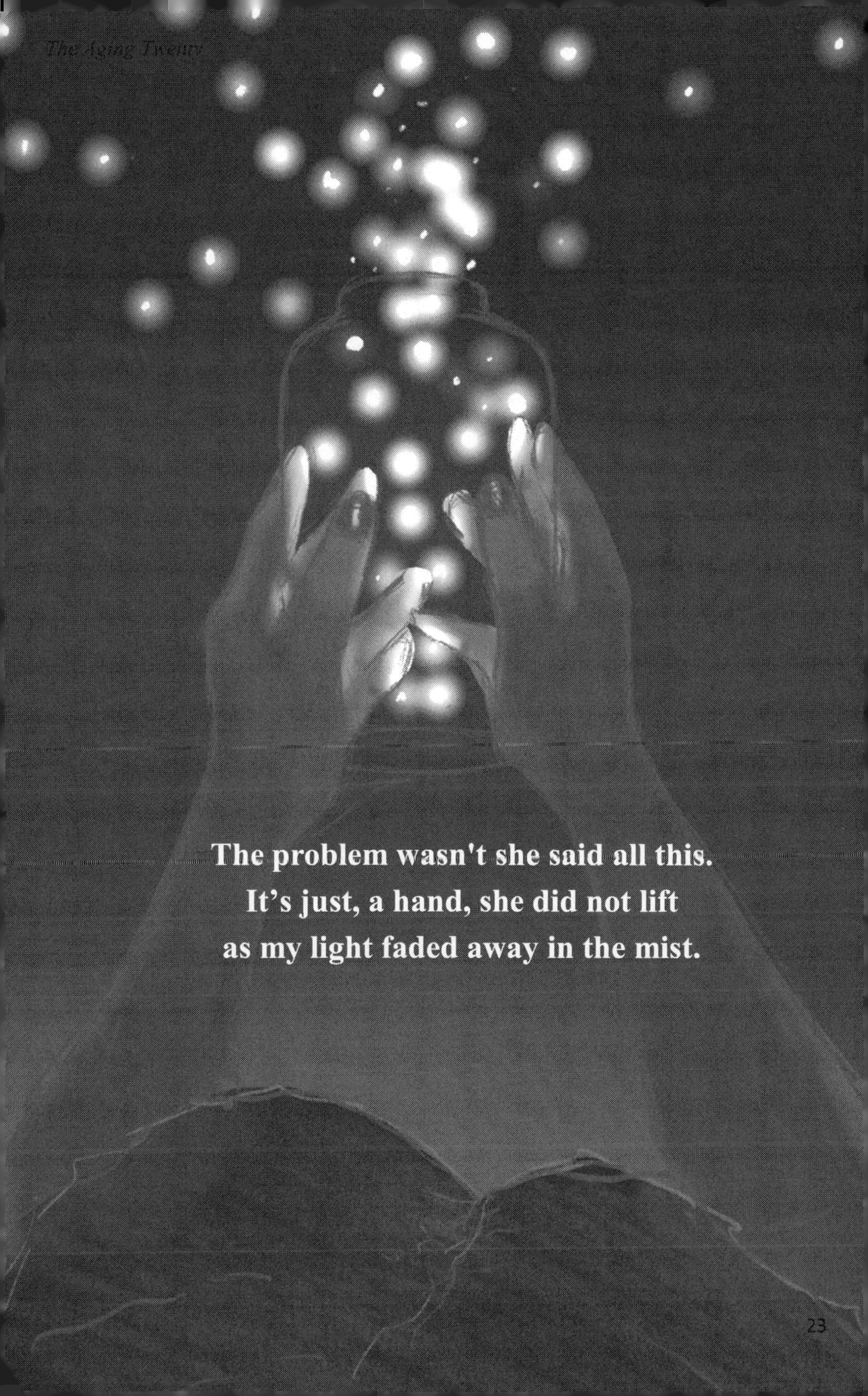

The problem wasn't she said all this.
It’s just, a hand, she did not lift
as my light faded away in the mist.

Random Noise At Night

I'm scared…
Why are you afraid?
You have something beautiful to say.

Do you know what you have to offer
Could be exactly what someone else needs...
Yes, but I'm afraid.

I'm scared that,
they gon' know I'm scared.
I'm scared that,
they gon' know I'm frail.
No, I'm scared they
already know I'm weak.
And behind all these wise tales,
Is just empty speech.

Most days I live within His glory,
But some days I face defeat.

As I sit here, on the edge of my seat,
I'm scared.

I'm scared that,
The rise from the fall
Won't come from a perfect leap.
And when I fall in front of their feet,
I'm scared that they will see all these
imperfections in me.

I'm scared that they will see
I'm scared that they will see me.

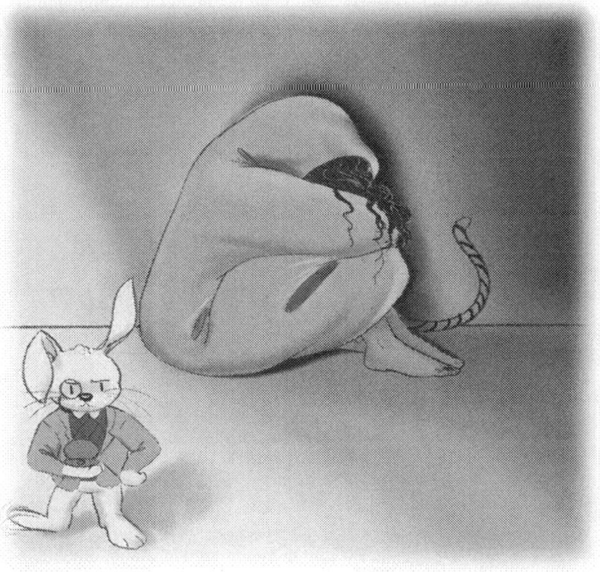

Doctor I'm Clinically Suppressed

I have good news!
Clinically you're not depressed.

Then why do I feel sad?

You just need some rest...
You've been through a lot that can cause
you stress.

Lady I'm dying! Of that I'm
positive.

Is there something you can give me? A pill of
some form?
An ol' wise tale? Maybe a rapid cure?
::Sighing::
As I left through the door

Stopping at the coat rack before glancing back
She gives a small corporate pat on the back.

Your fine, I promise that.

So, I re-adjust my mask
As she sent me out like that.

Since then, nothing else made sense.

Dress Rehearsals

I couldn't escape
this self-fulfilling prophecy.
A beauty among tragedies

I played an:
Unrehearsed,
Poorly written,
Screen playwright.

In which,
The master of my mind would string,
Ever changing scenes
Of individual concepts of my success.

Until my stage fright
Began to make me feel unease,
I was filled with interrupting climaxes

To only shake hands with the devil.
Nevertheless, I'd stand
at my curtain, awaiting
to see them again.

Store Brought

I picked a flower at the sto

Brought it home for it to glow
Had great expectations for it to grow

Put it in a vase,

sat it on my chase

The only thing I received was, less
growth

As her petals would fall

I would clean them all

Meanwhile, wondering, when she
took swipes at my throat

But, I brought a flower from the sto
and all she did was cry and croak

Rose

Like a precious rose
I protected you from much, the way

I wanted others to treat me as such.
I'd treat and re-treat your soil again and again.

Leaving your soul refreshed over springs of rain.

Each passing season; strength you'd gain,
to build up the courage,
to leave me again...

Window Garden Flower

Everyone seems to think that she
was a beauty in the rain
A constant shower she could take

Her consistent frostbitten limbs would not break
because for some reason she looked
like a beauty in the rain.

People would stop to smell her array
give notice to her in the summer amongst
the plain

But no one gave this beauty a break.
No longer could her petals stand up to
the rain

So in time, they began to sink
towards other lost warriors on the plain
where gravity
relieved her of her pain.

The Drought Always Came

I sent out my roots
To drink from a stream
They returned wilted to me.

So, I prayed for rain
Until flowers bloomed
But summer always came.

Test it would, well watered trenches,
Wintery nights and treasured blooms
But, the drought always came through

Lingering heat during the day
Nightfall her only break
She gave birth, forming full strength

Testing away my faith
Through the seasons
One promise remained,
The drought always came.

Chapter 2

Moving Furniture

Moving Galaxies

Piano

He used to
Rob my soul
Every time he
Played her piano keys

Strings of my heart
Would harp
As veins stayed their course
Breathless cells grew
Wings as they filled
The chambers of my heart

They would all agree
Every time he
Played those keys
Indeed he would revive me

Tea After Dinner: Love

I was attracted to you, your qualities; but
that's not what made me stay

It was watching you stand
In such obvious imperfection,

Through it all you would grow
So within your imperfections

I loved you so

Falling Stars

I had been aware I was standing
but hadn't noticed
the fall of sweetly amused stars,

and their little beating hearts,
moving in expectation of lovers from afar.

So, he kissed me where the moon met a star,
as the sun aligned together

We became as one heart, that is until,
Our solar eclipse begun.

Toni M. Goldwire

Star Gazing

Laying abroad
Where the moon danced
Jubilantly with the stars,

Slowly we built a home in each other's arms,
At times I couldn't figure out why,
Rhythmic beats would skip to distant qualms,

Or how every once in awhile
The new place, that I was fond of,
Lacked adequate oxygen and space in your arms

Leading me to deter inhalations of you,
For fear I would drown,
And overdose in your charms

Our love rendered diamonds,

but even diamonds have their

imperfections

Record Player

It's a recurring thing,
That you subject me to tears on my face.

Patient I was with this pain,
Until one day I distanced myself away.

Abandoning memories we had, I laid to waste
You and I, we walk as strangers in our place.

I didn't want to leave the thought of you,
So I ignored the hate that I held inside.

Which held me back from lashing out,
Simply because I couldn't say goodbye.

Now I sit here in silent rage, wondering
So silently I cry

If we reunite, will the pain subside?
Or will it make me die,

Because I don't have the courage,
To say goodbye.

Chemical Romance

She slams her pencil down. It falls
upon the elusive blue lined notebook;
Instantly he looks up.
In frustration she screams,

This chemical reaction is not balancing!

His quizzical brow from across the table
Stares in amazement at her lack of commitment
After all these years.

Staring out the window she blurts out a lie...
How she's tired and can't focus today

Somethings just not right.
These hydrogen and oxygen molecules have to balance,
They just won't align.

Kindly he looks, then states,

No two problems are alike, you have to make changes
For something to finally arrive.

A+ B= C, she yells teary-eyed, it's a straight line,
There are no other patterns or formulas that will align.

Let me see, he exclaims,

Taking the notebook that has caused so much disarray.
His eyes roll over, it's plain.
Then he says,

What's the definition of chemistry?

She rolls her head out of her hands and says...

Uncertainty.

Ok, now do the problem again.

Are we looking at the same problem on the page?

Don't you see that these electrons should not be float-
ing in mid air,
And these protons and neutrons, no matter what I do,
they repel.

As she reworks the problem intently,
He observes how her textbook formulas
Spill across the page, at different angles and curves.

Have you forgotten the basics of this…

What's a proton?
That's not a neutron.
The things you formulated is a living lie,
Formulas and symbols can't be changed.

It comes from the textbook!, she exclaims.
I hate this stuff...
As she turns her head up.

Worriedly he asked,

Define chemistry.

She whispers without looking up...

Uncertainty.

If the definition of chemistry is uncertainty,
That you hate so much.
Then what's the definition of love?

Uncert—

Tissues Are Proof

When the day keeps you from falling
But it's the night that keeps on calling

Tell me, who are you hiding from?
I'm stuck here in your wilderness

People tell me to just move on
That I cannot do although I can go back

I'm far to invested in the crescendo
So I just stay where you are

Every time I doubt how I changed
The space between us begins

So to the night I run
As she comforts what's been done

I feel it's only me who can stand beneath your sky

It's just a lie I tell

Which soothes me in the bed I lie

If I stay in those hues of greys
I will lose myself certainly

When I showed courage
I checked out of you to be free

Funny, that's when our love grew
When nothing was left to profess, protect or prove

All seems so cruel...

That I'm uncertain of tomorrows proof
And I'm scared I'll have nothing left

Wilted Rose Petals

I should have waited—
before falling in love.
To love myself first
is the wiser choice
than to see myself
wilting away in lust.

Broken Wine Glasses

I'm wondering, why
I blamed it all on you
All my feelings

I guess it's
You know the reasons, why
I cried, why
I feared, why
I can't sleep at night
And I guess, why
I'm here

That's why
you tried to
breath me back to life
But the only thing
you could breath
was toxicity

So now you know
The death of me

House Plant

How is it that you didn't notice this flower
standing on her feet?
How is it that you didn't notice this flower
blooming at her peak?

The same reason that you couldn't notice
her veins were slowly stiffening
Or petals falling and withering at your feet

And for some reason you couldn't notice
her smile was no longer glistening
So when shc sang, you stopped listening,

But there was something she noticed, that
YOU didn't care about me
Unless my beauty could serve you continu-
ally

So tell me, how is it you didn't notice, this
flower dying standing on her feet

Nice Talk

Even when your
Narcissistic lies crowd my faith
Still, slightly,
I want to believe emotions on your face
Even when your eyes painted behind deep disguise
tell the story of how deep our love lies,
I still almost believe your face

Not a brow unmatched
Not an emotion unchecked
Without a coordinated grasp
On body languages mask.
You seize my weakness,
light to my darkness,
the thing that helps me maintain
my hope in humanity.

Even when people have cursed
and shamed my name
I still have hope that they'd change.

So, that's where you reside,
Even when I know you lyin'
a small part of me still wants
to believe you'll change

The worst part of it all is
Even when I know you lyin'
A small part of me still wants to
oblige

Date Night

"You're too pretty to cry"…
Sir, I'm sorry but,
Tears don't discriminate
Against which soul to flow.
They condensate;
Until they gain enough strength
To travel their road,
Collecting at the chin.
Dropping as a dagger to the heart;
Just to condemn it again.

Dinner: Asking for Seconds

“I'm not ok,
How can you ask me that
When you see my face”.

Just then I grieved,
Tears ready themselves to race
Down a face that asks,
“What do you know
About the darkness?”.

I can't ask you for comfort,
That would require a soul
In order for empathy to take place.
You noticed my soul disappearing
Awaiting for your help or grace,

I sat there two minutes away– from death
And all you did was indulge in yourself.
I was two minutes away– from
and all you did was indulge in yourself.

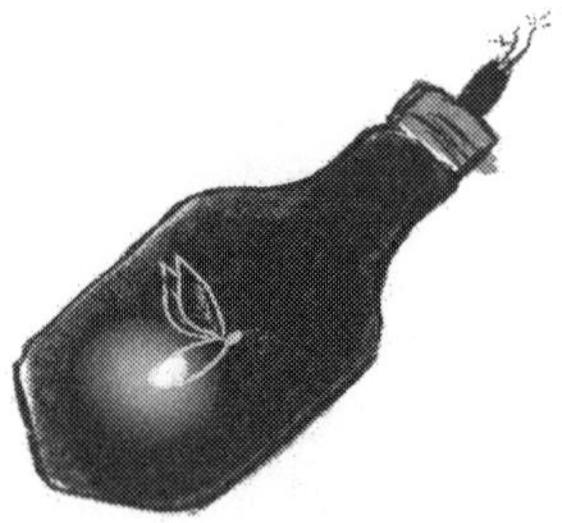

Chapter 3

Light Bulbs

Sofa

As you sit, you're so far
Away from the heart you now hold
Saying you'll go
But I tell you,
"Just hold on...
Can you stay here?"

Until the moonlight has let go?
And morning has resurrected
What happened on this sofa

If you go,
please don't go so far
If you leave,
there will be no moonlight
To see me
Sitting, crying, on this sofa
If you go,
please don't go so far away

I don't know

How long I can wait

Wondering why you couldn't stay
I just wanted you here for one more next
Season we'd spend at each other's necks
At least we'd be comfy on this sofa that way
And you'd still be here

I could've stopped you but we were just too far
So, every time you go
I sit here crying on this sofa
Awaiting on your return... again

Cat Naps

It's the only place I can go without shame
To see your face which hasn't changed.
Emotions on it which I evoked;
No matter how fast I run,
I never seem to make it to your side...

How is it that tears come down
Every time I dream I cry,
Translating these tears into reality, now
They Beg me not to wipe them down
'Cause recently we've cut ties
And if I do, I'd lose you, somehow

As you pushed, I pull you closer,
It's the only way to see your smile.
I pushed, through these nightmares advances
I never expected that once I reached you,
I'd slip through your grasp somehow...

How is it that tears come down
Every time I dream I cry,
Translating these tears into reality, now
They Beg me not to wipe them down
'Cause recently we've cut ties
And if I do, I'd lose you, somehow

Can someone tell me, how
Tears come down
Every time I'm close to you, how
I want to sleep to see your face, how
My tears cry out begging me not to wipe them out,
'Cause I'd wake from this dream somehow.

Hallmark Cards: I'm Sorry

Although my heart is beating
I no longer believe in...

The burning flames are starting
To ask if you think of me,
If not, why not?

As I reached out of your perfect storm
You pulled me down
And everyday I'm bleeding under this smile

But all you said was...
Sorry.
I no longer accept her now.
But all you said was...
Sorry.
I no longer accept her now.
The last time I did,
It almost took me out

Although I'm through with all the sor-
ries
You left my heart on her bed
Calling out… hear it calling now

The winds of its neglect, just tumbling
down
As I reached out, all you did
Was pull me down

And now your...
Sorry.
But we don't believe her now.
And now you say your...
Sorry.
But we don't believe her now.

Luggage

He watched her every move,
But she knew.
When she'd walk in or leave a room
she knew.
He noticed the change in her pitch and
the different way her heels would
click,
But she knew.

His eyes, he knew
were the one thing she could never
lift,
But she knew.
If she looked back, she could
never retract and that

She Knew

She Knew

Shower

Taking a cold shower is just
a reminder,
that the world is cold.

Scorching hot, to burn my skin
I'm just trying to resurrect what's within,

Warmth– is what I'm trying to gather in.
For the coals of my soul to reignite,
A recollection of how love is.

Maybe, it's just hard to keep pretending
because of you I'm not here again.

Winning: Agreements in the Shower

Tell me something, isn't she the one you adore?

Then why you leave hear standing there for

Emotions left on her face

For another man to come and explore

why she's falling,

down the path

that you left

her for.

She's crawling

sweeping the ground,

what's she looking for?

Something foreign

To rise out of her darkness

And heat up her life

So she can breathe in life

She'll just hold on, this close to the ground

Until she gathers her pride
Within her rattles now
Within her rattles sorrow
Within her battles now.

House Fly: Unwanted Guest

Because of you, who left me
My thoughts are no longer concrete
I can’t do anything without you, so
I stay home.

Because of you, who left me
I can't go without the security, that
My heart won't buckle at its knees
In doubt from listening to thoughts, that you
May not come back to me.

When they mention your name, tears
Collect until they begin to stain each cheek
until my resolve becomes weak.

Between the Two: Telephone

He dialed my number

I answered alarmed,
Knowing what he wants.

This time he didn't talk
He just left me a song.

Just a reminder that,
we both hold broken hearts.

I Can't See

I can't seem to see, opening my eyes
Still, I can't seem to see

These tears are smoke in my eyes,
I can't seem to wipe photographic
memories away

Blink as I try the blur in my eyes
wash up late versions of, you and I

I can't see past the sea of my decon-
structed soul,
Too broken to hold—

Hope

So, my tears waver on my lids
Just lacking…discipline.

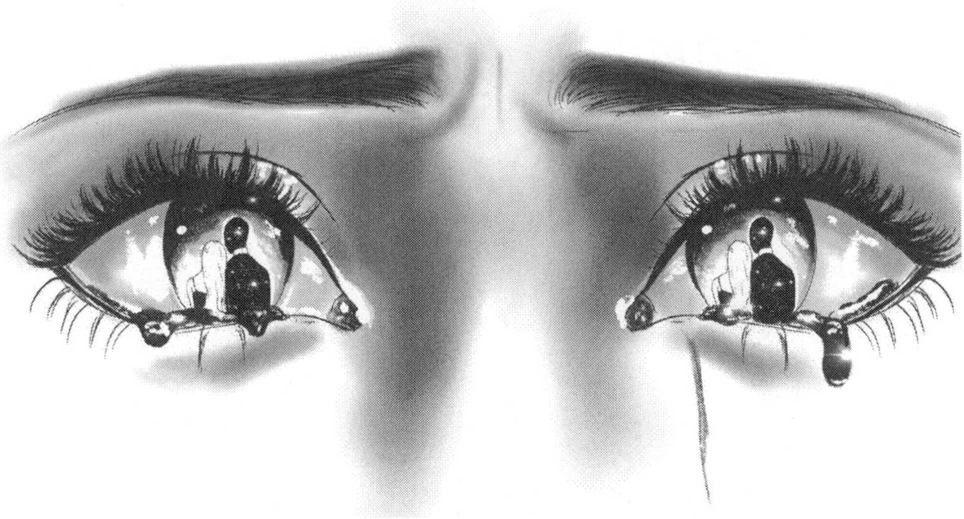

I made a logical decision;

But my heart hasn't

caught up yet.

Coffee

When the window pane calls her name,
she goes to exchange sips of coffee at the cafe again.

But this time she feels something strange.
Perhaps, the filter was loose again, so she's tasting those grains that floats within.
Just one more thing for her to regret.

Still, steam rises from the cup in her hand.
As she wonders did she put too much sugar in. That could be why it didn't go as planned.
It was supposed to be a little boost, a little something to lift the wings of sin.

Suddenly, she realizes coffee doesn’t taste the same without him.

After an ending,
There is a beginning,
An unfamiliar place—
An empty space
In favor of you losing faith

CHAPTER 4

UNFINISHED ROOMS

Rage
Is pain
Left over time.

Blanket

He wrapped up the waters from my tears
Storing them in the clouds that lay near
Maintaining them until the day was clear
To rain upon the earth

The quakes of my fears
Pummeling down the dust
Watering vegetation it had birth
Tears laid, splashing between
My heaven and his earth

Strange it all seems
For me to mourn my heaven
While sitting on God's turf

Praying For Anger

Now what,
do I pray for anger,
to get over my fear?
All the while,
praying for frustration
to get out of pain?

It all ends the same,
It simply leads to a long line of R.A.G.E.
So, I think I'll pray for anger to mask the pain

Kneeling here I'll pray
for moments in the past.
And for masking another day
in this indignant state.

In this position I'll stay
Until I think of something else to say
But, as for today
I'll pray for the anger to stay

Current prayers on fire:

Love

Trust

Forever

Us.

Brushing My Teeth

Where am I to go Lord?
You said you wouldn't leave me in the pit.
Is that the way to build faith?
To go to the place, demons can't resist?
So, I guess I'll go there and sit.

The howling is done,
The wailing was fun,
And I've loafed about until I regret
gnashing my teeth until they're gums.

I saw this in a movie once,
If I ripped my garments maybe you'll come
To rescue, the way you did Jonah in the belly of the fish...
Or would that just leave you upset?

If there's a pounding of the chest
Without the heart and garments ripped apart as a set.
But lord, you yourself said, you wouldn't leave me in this pit.

There's a blessing in it

So,

Diligently I search

I know it's somewhere

I just can't see it when

I'm this deep in it

Thunderstorms

When it rains I edit;
All the things that bother me

Taking away apostrophes
Crossing out we, and adding me.
Commas replace, these stops; and
dashes— interrupt
Negative thoughts

So as the rain drops,
I'll edit my life away.
Proofread the past
Correct future drafts; the right way.
That's what I do when;
it's rainy like today.

Soup

Nothing quite cures a rainy day,
like soup in a bowl.

It makes you feel safe,
comfortable and warm.

Is there something like that for the soul?
Warms you inside out like a spring day,

A little something to shake the chill away.
I wish they made that for a day like today.

Coffee: My Second Cup

Sitting here drinking a second round of coffee
I feel you coursing through my veins
The owners think it's the double shot that has me shaking;

Truth is the past few weeks haven't been the same
So, to this coffee shop I came
I just needed one last shot

To remind me that everything
Without you now, is peaceful, serene

And the coffee running through my veins
Serves as a reminder that you're the reason
My heart palpated in pain

Realizing I no longer have the strength
To breath between empty spaces

While I wait for morning coffee to hit
my stream

Caffeine is my reminder,
Not to drink of you again

Running Errands

As I stood in line at the market yesterday
I saw the side of your face...

My entire body stopped,
As my heart reached out,

My hands stayed in place, but
My eyes wanted to shout.

As I stood in place, standing
in the market place line that day…

My lips froze in between the space
Of pronouncing your name, and

The things you did wrong yesterday
So my heart began to race.

Theoretically, I reached for your grace,
Only to the side, my hands, remained

With my hips gridded in heavy restraints.
My feet grew dull to walking your way

For even,
my body knew

walking towards you,
would be a mistake.

Chips
Chips!
chips
Chips
Chips!
6PCK

Chips
Chips
G G G

Checking In

Am I looking for an excuse to get out of
my head?
Or am I tired of feeding the clouds of
dread?

Am I looking for a love I could never
have?
Or am I just a perfectionist in the
crowd?

Am I adjusting to his every command?
Or am I losing myself again?

Am I looking for the one that I truly
love?
Or am I in love with the idea of being
loved?

Am I really a hopeless romantic?
Or am I just lonely on this planet?

Am I afraid to be alone?

Or am I too weak to face myself on my own?

Am I secure in your love?

Or am I drowning in your uncertainty?

Am I losing in my journey?

Or am I in need of a break?

Am I faithless?

Or am I just exhausted?

But wait,

Am I…

Faithless?

Firefly

In the twists and turns of your lost plight
I took refuge in you during the night

Illuminating wings, you'd glare
Sweet short synapses of when we were there

Endearing moments no one else could share
In reigned your darkness of little light

Those dark moments made it clear
There was nothing stirring my heart here

Running Man

I feel so far away.
Run to him, he said.

I'm not sure if he'll even listen after all I did.
Still run ahead.

I can't even stand, from my heart's dreads.
Turn to him instead.

I'm tired of lifting my hands.
I'll hold them up for you; don't fret.

I can't approach his throne, I'm unworthy in my head.

Walk with me, I'll hold your hand.

With Him

She no longer asked for:
Wisdom
Nor to understand

Those things were sand in her hand.
Although, entities fought, and she wanted to rest,

In order to pass the final test
A Disciplining love needed to finish her quest.

Enduring his clarity,
she would have to withstand.

So the only thing left, was,
to leave it with Him

T. Goldwire LLC

Instagram: @ToniMGoldwire

Website: https://tmgold87.wixsite.com/tonimgoldwire

Merchandise: https://toni-m-goldwire.myshopify.com

For the Reader

Do you remember...? My friend would often ask. To be honest with you, I don't remember much of 2017. I remember the beginning when I lost my grandmother in death and the end when I thought I lost my mind. I believe mentally I blocked that year, so I didn't have to remember the painful memories. Epiphanies were key to my growth and getting through that tough time.

I realized emotions are the one thing that can connect and disconnect us at any given moment. While going through my own unique set of challenges, I realized I'm no different from anybody else. Love, joy, and fear are natural. We all deal with bouts of depression, anxiety, fear, and pain. These are the very things that make us human.

All too often we are told that vulnerability is a weakness. When in actuality, it's where we find our greatest strength and our biggest connection with others. Honoring these emotions is important as it is the only way to learn to love ourselves.

Today, I still don't remember much of that year, but ironically, I remember the day I started writing this book. It was all I could do to ease the pain. I felt like I was losing my mind, there were so many things I wanted to say but couldn't because no one would fully understand.

Hence, I wrote for the brokenhearted, the depressed soul, the lowly of heart, the misunderstood, the anxious and the one without a voice. In some hope that they would be able to identify themselves in this collection and know that, although now it's tough, they will make it in this journey. So, don't lose faith in the process, because the process requires faith.

Sincerely,
–T.Goldwire

People I'm blessed to have in my life:

My Family

Roseann P.

Sabrina B.

Devona H.

Thank you for all the love and support you've shown me over the years. A word of encouragement at the right time, a strong swift kick in the butt, a hand at the right time, and a shoulder to cry on. You kept me going and believed in me even more than I did my-self at times. Thank you and I love you! Gracias y te quiero mucho!

My supporters and extended family:

For every show, reading, ticket, book, click, like, re-post, forward, and review. I want to say thank you! All of your continued support and kind words encourage me to keep writing. I love all of you. I wouldn't be able to do what I do without you guys. I promise I won't keep you waiting too long for the next one!

If I was blessed to meet you along the way in my journey so far, we met for a reason. Either it was a lesson or a blessing, or a good laugh or a gut-busting cry. Either way, I am thankful to you all.

Made in the USA
Columbia, SC
02 January 2025

50994009R00065